HINDSIGHT

-Indelibles tattooed on my middle finger

Henna Quill

Published in the United States by KCG Publishing,
an imprint of Kuumba Creative Group, LLC, Ohio.

Library of Congress Control Number: 2021930115

ISBN: 978-1-7363405-0-9 (Paperback)

Photography by: Jehan Daugherty
Photography Model: Shanna Dean
Graphic Design & Interior Layout by: theEdWeb

www.KCGPublishing.com
info@KCGPublishing.com

First Edition

KCG Publishing

Acknowledgements

With every fiber of my being, I thank:
God, my ancestors & transcended loved ones, myself,
my children, grandchildren & future fruit, husband, parents, grandparents,
business partner, business accountability partners (BAPs), family and close friends,
wine timers & other pre-readers, publishing coach, photographer/model, and graphic designers.
This project is exceptional because of you, your ideas, and your commitment.
I love, respect, and appreciate you. This win is all of ours.

Dedication

To those who have been called *thirsty*,
in both the best and worst possible ways …

For Hindsight, you truly are 20/20.

Table of Poems

Part I: Autumn

Part II: Winter

Part III: Spring

Part IV: Summer

Part I: Autumn

Visionaries

Let us journey,
    figuratively
Let our minds walk
among the garden
of prosperity
Let our lips
preach
Let our figures
journey

Hindsight

He was beautiful
like a riverbank, lush
with possibility. I welcomed
him like a drink after a long walk
in the aridness of solitude.

He was charismatic. Drawing
me into three-hour conversations
on topics I cared nothing
about: boxing, bowling, and such.

His charming ass even recited the
Solemnization of Marriage Address
before consummation.

"Dearly beloved we gather here
to witness the union of these
two souls in matrimony…"

It all felt as lovely as
having car and restaurant doors opened
for me, like coming home
to a candle-lit
bath with hyacinth petals,
and Joe's *All that I am*
streaming from the stereo.

But over time, his beauty
eroded. Six-months to the date,
the face of truth emerged.
Skin a complexion of malevolence,
eyes glazed in wickedness,
and a mouth contorted
ill-intently.

His lyrical charisma
a manifest extension
of him. His
tongue lashed, verbally
whipping my ass.

"You stupid Bitch!"

Flagrantly
staccato, his words
were compositions
of harsh melodies
like knuckles pounding
on piano keys.

"You're a fucking waste of DNA!"
disfigured my integrity,
suffocated my serenity,
and annihilated any balance
of sensibility.

And I stayed off tilt for four years. I'd
tongue-kiss my case of vertigo
between bouts of oral malice.
And I tried to make it love me.
But it only made me too dizzy
to leave.

Now, I am sheathed in scathing
afflictions; emotional scabs
that cleft with every breath
of memory.

I would not be
had Hindsight shared her wisdom
that this love
was to be foregone.

So, I am convinced.

Hindsight is an agent
of ridicule, insulted intelligence,
and assaulted discernment.

Hindsight is Time's whore.
She prostitutes the Present.
She solicits herself at the crossing
of intuition and ignorance.

And I can't tell if she is too chicken-shit
or just too damn dumb
to be like Foresight
and at least bust one during the fuck.

So, the Future pimps her.
Bitch-slaps her to lull
her Johns
into inebriated stupors.

Hindsight is a bitch.
And I want to kick her ass. Bruise
her with the same shame
and inadequacy
that shrouded me
because she did not
have the courage
to open her
fellatio-serving mouth.

Soul Mate

My ears listened
to the rich baritone
notes streaming out
from the waters
residing in the depths
of you. Visions filled
my eyes. I could see
us nurturing love; pure, full.

My eyes caressed your body
while my mind tasted
the delight
of your thick liqueur.
One glass made me
mellow. The next
made me babble
non-senselessly,
uncontrollably.

It was familiar…
I have known its taste
since I was nothing
more than a mere thought. I know
its strength; potent and undiluted.

Thought, spirit, flesh,
babe, child, adolescent, woman.
See time swirled around me
like racing atoms. Yet the memory of you
remained within me
as vivid as the pain
of your absence. I never forgot
your taste. Never forgot
the number of glasses I need
to reach that sublime level of
ecstasy.

So, I sought out after you. I searched
in vessels varying in design, color, shape.
Each answered to a different name,
each's composition only a variation
of a theme, each lacked
the combination of ingredients
that I longed for,
found only
in your thick liqueur.

Finally, along came you,
a strong black vat. When you poured
your contents over me,
I was whole again.

This Is a Lust Poem – Sort of

Tonight, we united mouths for the first time.
Standing in the rain
glaring at each other.
Spectacular forces
gently drawn together
by the electromagnetic energy
that blankets us. Before
you, I have never been kissed in the rain.

I was impressed
by the way that you pulled
me close and enveloped
me in your embrace.
Rain drizzled down on us
from the sky
like little drops of destiny.

I became lost
in your mouth and I slipped
from myself
for one quaint moment.

In that quick lapse,
I realized
that I breathe
love when your cologne is near; deep,
warm, smooth musk.
Your aroma fills me.
Your scent is my sustaining breath.

I feel love when your slender hands
wash upon and wave
over every inch of my land.

You lead me to acknowledge
what lives
at my core…
a mouth overflowing
yet thirsty.

If I Had My Way

If I had my way
I would let you have yours
I'd let you have all of me … all of me.

If I had my way
you'd tuck inside of me
every night, accompany me
to starlight galaxies
unbound by clocks, maps, or DNA.

We'd be
transcendents doing what transcendents do
transcendents transcending transcendentally
we'd be
while you thick tucked inside of me.

And when the breathless universe
recesses from its quiet
whispers of clarity
alive and awake again
once more
you rouse me with your mouth
acquainting me
with the gift of a new day.

Good Morning Sweetheart
rolls raspy from your lips, juicy like sauce.
Your words tantalizingly fondle my ear
and I can't imagine you being anywhere but here
tucked deep, deep, deep inside of me.

The Rain Philosophers

We waited
    evaluated
our compatibility

We wondered
    unknowingly
Pondered and contemplated
our oneness

We definitively came to know
that to have one soul
is to be rain descending
parallel
from heaven to Earth
mating on the pinnate leaves
of mahogany trees

And we were right

And although often
thoughts form
in my head and finish
on your lips, after the sex deluge
halved to a drizzle
things became strange between us

Our days now labor
like droplets strained
in an hourglass narrow
and limbo lazily lingers
lapping up time
like a languid labrador

We now view our nakedness
as a cohesive bead
clinging

with hesitant suspension
of anticipation,
unaware
of the duration
of its seemingly eternal
dissension

And we are still right

Love's Cradle

…and we are so careful now

We cradle this new love as
fragile as a pre-mature birth

We walk slowly
when a time ago
we would have run

We talk long
and pause
in between
to think
 to reflect
  to see
   clearly
…no hasty impulsiveness now
as like in the days of old

We cradle this new love
We cradle this new love

Love's Bell

Love is a bell with swelling
and diminishing
sound; a pendulum
of kinetic loudening
and quieting.

Lovers' conjectures – capricious
ebbs and flows of waves
both synergistic and stymied
– are the cadence
of the carillon.

And at the toll of a bell
is the sexing
of its clapper
with each side
both left and right.

Neither side true
nor false,
just subject rather to one
outcome
or another.

Love is a bell, is a bell
non-linear; for it is not a singular
serpentine inclining, peaking,
and declining; but a tale

of two transients
at the zenith
of their journeys
sharing their experiences
from each side
of the ascension.

Hesitation

In your eyes,
I see possibility;
though your voice is weary
and your heart
seems tarnished.
This new love that I carry
in my womb is the polisher
that you
desperately need.
This truth,
this faith
that I bear in me
is yours to accept.

belly plucked

belly plucked from dust
and god's breath. screaming
breech to cease. restore me
to warmth, familiar.

heaves stop breath
newfound anyway.
hysterical, demanding understanding,
why this disruption?

warm mounds, milk scented.
bob around till blissful suckle.

this birth is universally ours,
traumatic but not tragic.

yet, there are men dividing the earth.
causing pain and shame.
raping bodies, raping souls.
phallic symbolism ramming
sacred, flesh-moist war grounds.

bayonets, broken bottles, bullets,
and hardened soldiers
with calloused hearts insert
where innocence dwells,
instead of intimate swells.

innocence now a wandering ghost,
untimely departed from her; too confused,
too betrayed to rest.

so many phalluses, so violent
that her tears claw
at earth's cervix,
demanding
the dust to open
that she may crawl back in.

inversions

in the gallery of a small unknown place
the dawn-break exhibition of my mind
inside the space of chalk outlines
murdered portraits once occupied
now mute mutilated hues promulgate

a world inverted
where the bowels
of the deep
groan in the heavens
and loose earth
sloughs off as rain

where stars scatter the ground
like bar fight broken glass
and the loose trash litter of clouds
line unkempt streets
stray bullets are shooting stars

and there is no sun only lunacy
the moon also relegated to the abyss
slices its lunar light up
through dehydrated layers
of cataractous waters unevenly
meting itself
over the deathscape

anchored between
the likes of feces and urine
is a shovel-shaped island of earth
shattered skulls and bony phalanges
flipping the bird
pepper the shore
and the stench
of societal spoils –
values, principles, convictions, and such
is death's wrist eau de parfum

in the open mouth of day
all inhabitants ritualize
orgies of perversions, murder, and genocide
save for in the un-sovereign shadows
where the righteous reside
in anarchy
we do not murder,
do not forcefully sex take,
nor corrupt the minds
of our young
yet, we are considered terrorist
when we witness
with our moral tongue

wordsmithery

it is weaving words on looms
into concepts
clear, concise, and succinct.
fashioning thoughts
into luxurious silk
to adorn beautiful
bodies.

it is laboring
to stitch words together
with perfect seams,
neat and tight enough
to convey
the precise image
in your head.

it is choreographing
words to move
like perfect
executions of ginga, rolè, and au
movements – translating
the power, art, and fight
of Capoeira.

it is layering words
into compositions
that whisper to babies,
console dying souls,
and belt out truths
real and raw –
sounding sirens,
and awaking
the consciousness
of the walking dead.

it is the divinity of mating
words to birth
beautiful children.

ones that are smooth, ebony-skinned,
self-assured, and confident
of their potency.
sometimes mulatto
with curly hair,
and skin blended
beautifully enough
to entice questions
that beg
to be answered.

it is bathing words
in Holy water.
scrubbing them
until they reach spiritual purity
and become
sacred, vessels of cathartic release.
ageless, profound, full
of truth
and understanding.

it is the act of doing it
that i love.
also, the mature
and sometimes alzheimersed
thoughts produced.

Pas de Deux

Relishing in the acquiescence
of the sun,
the orderliness
of the sand, and
the compliance
of the water…

You shape English
into origami and calculus,
but mostly polarities
of black and white:

*"Religion for some is a mask, for others
it is a river without a bridge."*

I too sculpt English
into intellectually
brilliant wordscapes:

*"Yes, religion is the most beautiful
case of anemia."*

Inspired by you, I continue
to contribute
my gypsy tongue,
my dialogue tastes
of curry… paprika… cayenne pepper:

*"Sanity, the thing most desired,
is hellishly elusive. At best,
it is as far as the width
of an open field; at worst,
dimensions away, a labyrinth
of shattered mirrors."*

Your voice scratchy with irritation:

"Life is a portrait of light,
the cosmos is a mosaic
of every person's energy."

I express: *"How profound!"*

You stare me down
and dictate
that my *"energy is a black hole."*

Tsunami swells in sea's
belly. Water wall high,
spikes the sun
the from sky.
Drenched
of your urine; I
clear my eyes.

Polite bones –
"Did I say something wrong?"

****

Your easiness is remarkable
amidst the submissive
china,
the obedient
silverware,
and the maître d' eager to please
table 3.

You lark happy pour
wittingly into my ear
about how evolved you are
since your molars never developed.

I interpolate with naivety
and interject

unique-angled
thoughts of my own:

"Today's music is like
buying a box of cereal
full of screws, nuts, and bolts."

You assert:

"I admire your language mastery,
but I believe
that you enamor yourself
more."

Your tongue a torch
of flames, extinguishes
my fire.

Drenched
of your urine;
with seared eyes:

Polite bones –
"What the fuck
is wrong
with you, you
egotistical bastard?!"

Bonehead –
"What the fuck
is wrong
with you, you
narcissistic bitch?!"

Tattered Handshakes

Tattered handshakes aren't nothing
to hold on to, but there they are
my private dossier
of unwed salutations; filed, labeled,
and date stamped.

Of course, they never start
off the frayed carcasses
they become…

I greeted Johannes and Tariq with salsa
red-nailed jezebels – shea butter soft
and black amethyst perfumed.

The former and I
slipped tequila down our throats
and danced until our arches pained.
While the latter and I
never saw the other side
of my door jamb – not together at least.

Cordray and DeLance, those lucky bastards,
were of the golden era
of custom-tailored clothiers
and personalized diamond cufflinks.

Cordray and I globe-trotted the African Sahara,
while DeLance and I watched Broadway
shows like weekly sitcoms. Though, as plenary
as our lives were, neither chose to stay.

Shannon and Rolon, somewhat shortchanged,
were met with sinuous sapphires. Firm
with the sophistication of maturity, but supple
with the suggestion of womanly ache.

And we played house.
We followed the habitual script
to a T, right down to the working
of Sunday crossword puzzles
in bed.

But despite all
of my attractiveness, my cajoling,
my youthful seduction –
without regard
to the four sizes too big
confidence that I eventually grew
into – each tryst resulted in nothing
more than starch pressed stitch lines
of introductory pleasantries
and disappointing farewells.

I've catalogued so many
unemployed introductions
that even I am not impressed
with myself anymore.

At one point,
I even let my cuticles dry-out
and crack, left my nails unpainted,
and didn't mind
my worn-out
cuff hems.

I figured
I could
beat Murphy's law that way.
But Murphy, like the rest,
would make no commitment.

I wish I had
nothing to let go of. But I have

this flotsam of tattered handshakes, that I hold
on to like one day I will
decipher the common thread
of their truth.

Intangible

I cannot touch you,
intangible. Transparent
bastard.
Plastic ring, imaginary marriage.
You married your own life
while I vowed
to the thought of you. Your flesh
unavailable. You are
intangible, non-reciprocal,
expressionless, emotionally void.

Loneliness, frustration,
endurance-less longsuffering.
I am cocooned in a state of hopeless
sobs, wrenching cries,
and creative alibis
for why you reject me
the way that you do.

I try to rationalize
and justify
why, but in the end
I find no reason
that I must suffer
this endless season
of living loveless
and remaining
faithfully true
to a selfish, predictably
unpredictable notion
like you.

Concede

If I shut the door to the burgundy '89
New Yorker, so help me God
do not let the engine start.

Flying, flying,
speeding
to nowhere,
recklessly
trying
to reach you.
yet, the distance remains
unchanged.
the distance is constant.

So, I stop
thinking of you,
I turn off your channel.
If I cannot reach you,
then it is best to leave
well enough alone.

It is best to bury
my fantasies.
Fantasies flowering a casket
of empty hope,
wishful thinking sprinkled
on the satin head rest pillow.

Cyclical Irony

It seems that all the words that I long to say
flatly slip away
whenever you are near
I tend to quicken my trot when I really
wish to slowly waltz into eternity with you.

Ironically, creative conversations escape
me in your presence, but imagination
is endless in my thoughts of you.

The hardest part is the uncertainty
that accompanies this silence.
Lonely, unending, unknowing.

You are so beautiful.
You must have someone
to love
you
must be the apple of someone's eye.

I do spy you from a distance, I try
to relinquish myself from rehashing
cyclical daydreams of our potential future
and I do manage to forget you
until I remember you again, see you again, repeat.

The Place Where Decisions Labor

11:00 p. m.
We bicker back and forth like someone chewing steak
too tough for one side alone to bear the burden.

In the beyond-bedtime darkened hallway,
our children assemble silently outside our door
peering into the gaps of its perimeter where light escapes.

11:05 p. m.
We are far from exasperation, but ready enough to abandon
this tenuous argument, circumventing a maelstrom's birth.

And here at the crossing of the past and the future –
the place where decisions labor,

I thought to move the long arm on our clock back from 1 to 12.
Changing the angle on the clock's face
from a check mark on something completed,
to an angle not unlike a wish bone.

It was just like pushing the back button
on a CD player to replay a song that on the
first time through you concentrated only
on the rhythm, neglecting the lyrics.

11:00 p. m. revisited
I see new details, unsullied by the blindness of a moment.

I noticed that your eyes are not laced with as
much anger as I had originally thought.
Your hands are shaky with a nervousness that I had not detected before.

Your shirt bears sweat stains and shards of grass.
And I realized that I had not even thanked you for mowing the lawn,
had neglected to ask you what your day had been like.

And when those five minutes lapsed again,
the clock face read 11:10,
but I do not mourn those 5 minutes lost
in the place where decisions labor. No, not at all.

the intermediate senses

deafness. it doesn't stop him from hearing.
he perceives the beats, music's throbbing and thumping.
he turns on the boom box's power,
places his hands on the steely ribbed speakers,
and gives into the vibrations.

...and like him, poets live in the deafness of observance.

noticing that some write the number four by drawing the line first
before attaching the 90° angle like an appendage
signaling a right turn. while others angle then line.

...and like him, a poet's mien is that of blind tactility.

there is a desire to touch the seam
of semi-consciousness and slumber.
twilight lends itself to be held and examined
so one knows how the mind rapid cycles
tomorrow's to-do lists and preoccupies itself
with what you should have said
in today's disagreement with your boss, your wife.

slumber, relaxed of valerian cocktails, is tangible as well.
one is privy to know that the mind is cinematic,
a scrolling banner of subconscious anxieties.
evident by remembering that you dreamt of fish,
of falling, of being pursued.

but that space of transition between the two
is a butterfly unwilling to be caged.
and if one could ever master its elusiveness,
they'd point their index tactile corpuscle deep
into that precise moment like a surgeon studying
the *bundle of His* in the center of a gutty heart.

The Lesson

Your love means to me that I too can be free.
Free to live my dreams, to make them become reality.
I will achieve because I am becoming whole.
I see that you are in my life to help me grow.
You help me to see the world through lenses of neutrality.
You help me put the pieces of the puzzle together.

Your love is real; your love is true.
And since all of me wants to reciprocate the same to you,
I often felt as if I had to catch up to you.
I now see that I was making it overly tough.
I have learned that whatever I give of myself
freely, openly, and honestly, is enough.
Now, I do not have to be so hard on me.
Learning this lesson is the beginning
of learning how to love and receive love
unconditionally.

Losing You to Myself

I wasn't ready to accept the detumescence
of our relationship. Partially swaddled in un-ripened
resignation, partially cowering in the shadowy eclipse
of my stubborn unwillingness.

Reluctantly, I began to redirect my efforts
away from vain attempts to salve the tears
between us, to salvaging our friendship –
which too proved to be as hopeless
as a farmer's yield in a drought year.
Eventually, I bottomed out to just plain savage
thoughts of how I could come out
on top breathing while you choked
on regret slipped down your windpipe.

I must admit, the hardest thing to accept
was that the other woman was me.
The woman that you had perceived me to be
and then disenchanted, decided that I wasn't.

It was maddening to know that I couldn't compete
with her prescience, the perfect words for every situation
neatly tucked in the folds of her mouth,
readily accessible like categorized prized-winning recipes.

It was painful to see that you had confidence in her
but none in me. Somehow along the way it had diminished
with every argument, every time you concluded that I did not
support you.

And it was hard to accept that I didn't lose you to some svelte twenty-
something year old. You actually found comfort in my extra sixty
pounds and humored yourself with narrating the stories
of my stretch mark pageantry.

But right at the end, no matter how many times I'd clear
the pathway in the hall, removing your work boots, the
unread and reread newspapers, no matter how much I tried
to put things back in their place, there laid the detritus
of our relationship like an impossible obstacle course.

Broken

When they split the final time,
she knew it was the last.
There were plenty of false alarms,
but this was it –
a clean sever
like Cutco through leather.

He took her for granted.
He took for granted that she
would never leave.
The grief crushed him
like a building
on his chest.

She did not cry.
Not one tear for four months.
Her endless reserve was empty.
She had drained it for four years.

A Day to Fall in Love

That day, the clouds
were cradling the sun.
Creating the perfect ambiance
for two lovers
on a blanket
under a giant
oak tree.

That day, the wind
was relatively quiet,
whispering only enough
to wisp my hair
gently
across my cheek
as I faced my lover.

Tears for Those Who Cannot Cry for Themselves

We met twenty out of twenty-three monthly cycles ago
at the main library in the business and technology section.
He was the color of sweet potato pie with hair the color
of burnt pie crust. I was green twig fresh and he was thirsty.

I had never seen a man's eyes thirst for me that way; had
never heard a tongue lap for me like a parched canine
grateful for an unexpected oasis.

In a room full of information about fascinating human
advancements and world-changing technology, I
was the discovery most desired. I felt like a new celestial
body in the lens of a star gazer.

He courted me for months, taking me to restaurants
where he ordered our meals in the few French words that he had
memorized from high school and self-teaching tapes.

We talked politics and about the lofty dreams each of us aspired
to achieve. We moved in together after he sold me on the line –
"You are so special to me"

But soon thereafter, his tone changed from charming to alarming.
"I hate you" replaced *"You are so special to me."*
"You cannot do anything right" shrieked louder than
"You are so special to me."
"You stupid Bitch" seared my ears
that once purred when they heard *"You are so special to me."*

He did not use his hands to prune me.
Instead, he cut me mercilessly with ill-spoken words.

I had no understanding of when or why our paradigm had shifted.
What did I do wrong? I thoughtfully prepared dinners of shrimp
fettuccine alfredo, masterfully blended with olive oil and pesto,

even though it could trigger my shellfish allergy.

I laundered the loads of blacks, colors, and whites, and
weekly changed the linen sheets. I wrote little notes,
marked the bathroom mirror with red kisses,
and seductively arranged my perfumed lingerie
in his foul-smelling sock drawer.

I had grown accustomed to receiving a kiss, a grateful embrace,
or a gracious *"Thank you!"* but eventually I looked for nothing
in return except a harsh shout in my face.

And those three missed periods, were two six-week spans
where my breast grew swollen and tender, and my stomach
juices seeped up my throat. I think it was his fits of stress
that beat those babies out of me.

My spirit broke and I turned to the Bible. I found
comfort in the scriptures, especially Psalms 43:

> *Vindicate me, O God,*
> *and plead my cause against an ungodly nation;*
> *rescue me from deceitful and wicked men.*

From then on, every day, I reached a new level within myself.
Every day, I grew stronger and less tolerant of his abuse.

And on one windless, cloudless, remarkably
weather-less day, I arose and walked out of the apartment.
It was like a new day breaking forth from darkness.

I walked past our bellman and smiled at him. He smiled back at me
with an endearing smile and knowing eyes. I kept walking past
the corner bistro, and the neighborhood library. I kept walking
and began to pass things in my past, like that day in the library,
my first day of college, my fourteenth Christmas, nights
when my mom braided my hair and told me stories about my father –
who chose his other family over ours.

I was breaking free; I would soon erase this pain from my memory
like smearing a sketch off sweaty glass.

But the deeper into my past I traveled, the more labored my breathing
became, and I had no choice but to abandon my escape. My delusion
was wearing off like all anesthetics do, and I started suffering
from the sickness of sobriety. I became achy and stale-mouthed
like someone in withdraw.

He was blood thirsty, and I was bruised, broken, and dying
on a linoleum floor. He did use his hands to viciously prune me,
it was his fists that beat those babies out of me. That day was not weather-
less, the rain was pounding against the window, and the sky
was delivering tears
to the flowers
who cannot cry for themselves.

Baby

One Beat.
Another
(pause)
Merge
Two Lives Intertwined
Into
One
Heartbeat
Cry

Part II: Winter

Refuge

It was in August, that I came from dust.
My newborn body sheathed with soft brown skin.
My being spawned from parent's youthful lust.
I am the treasure conceived from their sin.

January breathes upon my shoulders.
Aging process of life almost complete.
Problems hurl at me the size of boulders.
Afflictions lay mockery at my feet.

June has sprung from winter's dry, crisp grass blades.
With stance broken, as the neck of a swan,
I walk with three feet in slow graceful wades.
My soul in slumber at the breech of dawn.

Upon my grave a whirlwind of taunt leaves,
Whistle and swirl brittle sighs of relief.

st. clair

stillness surrounds her. white flakes
drizzle across mahogany faces. tattered
orange-brown patchwork hangs
unevenly around her shoulders. her ragged
garments reflect
in the snow crystals below.

bitter whispers invade her protective
shield which cracks like glass
under harsh winter winds. hidden thoughts,
disguised as simple stares and murmurs,
crush her spirit like snow beneath
a pedestrian's foot.

she stands silent, still. waiting
with frozen emotions, stiff
as the cold blue body
found three blocks to the north.

these strangers encircle
her with their false aristocracy
and glares. these strangers
do not care about the burdens
that she bears.

burdens she does store secretly,
ridicule she does store secretly,
pain she does store discreetly.
yes, stillness surrounds
her concretely.

Winter's Dance

Playing in the fiery cold
there is no sound, save
the whispers of ice chips
splendidly swirling off silver blades.
Pressures and expectations
seem to blow away.

Frolicking gestures, displayed by both
ice and self, kindle warmth.

Time, is a string-less kite
and I, surrounded by this utopia,
imagine this life just a dance of play.
Looking upon one of God's enigmas,
I know when the sun sets, this world goes away.

The humble air complements by woeing,
my thoughts affected by the soft snow snowing.

Winter's Dress

Momma said, "*Baby, you can't wear that dress*
today, it's cold outside. It's winter, Baby.
It's Ohio winter, Baby."
I wanted to wear the dress.
And I did.

After the adrenaline
of my headstrong pretty
dissipated, then too left the shielding
keeping fierce Ohio winter at bay.
Her magnificent crystal
touched me. Pierced me
sword length through,
from heart to vertebra.

How can something so bitter
court the eye so strongly
with such splendor and hypnotic swirl?
How can cold saw and burn?

My legs, frostbitten sawed
off. My fingers seeking to
decipher the tingle of numbness.
My lips, painted frosty
light blue, form to whine…
which escapes
dry, crisp, and bladed.
Momma responded *"Baby, I wanted to dress you for this."*

Again, I whined.
She said, *"Think and do*
something else."
But I stubbornly minded
my own lament.
I whined, again and again.
Momma said *"Run, dance, warm yourself."*

But I, seemingly legless,
did not dance nor run.

I bemoaned.
Momma said *"I SAID, STOP*
focusing on the cold. Do something
else. Distract yourself
if you must. Do something
you love. At the very least,
do something
you don't hate.
Do what you choose,
but you will stop,
this whining and whining and whining."

I stopped my sniveling,
stopped my shivering,
stopped my shaking, and shaking, and shaking.
I had touched the stove,
got burnt by its flames.
I had made way for it.
I had,
had my way.
I had dressed myself
pretty. Done what I had. Done
what I had wanted
to do.

Momma hugged me tight,
wrapped my neck
with her old
orange-brown scarf
and led me,
led me inside,
towards the embers awaiting,
towards the comforting warmth
of a sundrenched summer
day.

Freedom for Women, Takes Time

I stayed because
I wanted to
fix what was broken. I was
waiting for the redo
of the undone.
I bent sway
to the familiarity
and convenience
that things must keep
to the travel
to the course
to the line
of the status quo.
If it ain't broke,
don't fix it.
If it is shattered,
be patient
because it will take slightly
more time.

It wasn't that he was
so good at the start. He wasn't
that good at all. He was nothing
at all
spectacular. He,
nor it, nor the time
between us two.

I stayed because
I hadn't yet learned
to unclench my fists,
to let go,
to make room.
It takes time for us.
It takes time for us
to let go.

Freedom for us takes time
by design; puberty, pregnancy,
and menopause all incubate
and brood.

Menstruate cycles monthly long
like the Earth cycles yearly round
the sun.
She periodically
comes undone
with the frequency of normal.
Young her must early bear,
in silence,
the burden
of silencing the oddity
of cyclical birthing and dying.
She must shoulder
the burden that it is
normal. Heave and carry
the burden of making it
normal, to exist
to live absent
of the crazy label affixed.

Monday returns,
January returns,
the first of the month
returns, but years
they do not. And when to close
the book on such a stretch of time
changes depending on the month
to which that stretch belongs.
How can one easily distinguish
the exceptions
from the rules?

Her existence marked,
by becoming

undone and redone
and undone and redone,
with sequential refrain.
This cyclical birthing and dying,
this contrasting and comparing
decodes for her
the rhythm of life's
coming and going,
it serves her
hint and clue.

While the boys
spared they are, are not
really spared at all,
only delayed, only lulled
into the falsehoods
of magic
of instancy
of the lie
that everything
resides outside of oneself
and can be forced to bend
with or without sway.

He sleeps soundly
during the incubating months,
whilst she tosses and turns, confronting
her muscles' stretching and tearing.
She feels the flutters
long before baby's
bones form enough
to flex for him, to hold his
stare, eyes wide
and startled. She feels
the burps, gases, and urine
releases inside herself
before they hear
baby's first verbal cry.

Her body,
overtime works to give
to what she grows.
Inward, her body expels so much
energy that outwardly
her skin glows.
And when her body
and what she grows within it
no longer agree to remain
that way, she sheds
all that her body has
worked to give away.

Over time,
time passes over,
and yet, another
moment presents
to become undone
and redone yet again.
To unsubscribe and resubscribe
from who she is
and from all
that she has
come to know
and from all
that she has
come to be
and from all
the ways in which
she normally
goes about. To trade
what she knows for something
else, something uncertain
and new. This time
fire hot and nearing final. Freedom
for women, takes time.

It is the spanning,
that keeps her
it is the spanning
that seasons her like sage.
It is the spanning
that gives her choice
to distinguish freedom from cage.

Her Eyes Spoke

Mute, mouth-occupied,
she advised with loathing eyes,
"...fill your empty spaces
with things that hold your attention –
the way your hand must
to conduct
the holding of your pen..."

Hymns for Those Who Did Not Make the Cut

In order ... to refrain ... breathe ... 1, 2, 3

[1] i think, I think in cursive.
String streams of consciousness.
Connect seemingly desperately, disparate things.
Thread their themes of common,
[2] i wander about,
thread- wandering
seems to seams.

Wondering,

pondering literary theorems,
christened with befitted names
of bespoke measurements.
Stitch if one-day adornments.
Hook blankets for swaddle.

Catchy hooks
catch and never let go.
Like this hook in my head,

[3] *"...fill your empty spaces*
with things that hold your attention –
the way your hand must
to conduct
the holding of your pen..."

"Cut once, think twice."
A safeguard to appraise
words that've leaked from my pen,
and to mind each one's posture,
sparing those that sharply cut-in
like brash solos tubing the harrowing
"I am worth saving."
i will not make the cut.

Every time I write with pen,
I am soothed within,
by the song of my own refrain,
a chorused string of lines
that were not cut.
again. refrain by refrain by refrain.

(in)sanity

you're the one with a label affixed to your palm,
whereby anyone who greets you
becomes aware of your personality disorder,
your abrasiveness, your unwarranted aggressiveness,
your unrealistic yardsticks, your uncanny
ability to shape a saint into a sinner,
to slither yourself into a place of superiority.
you're the one who should be littered with bottles
of antipsychotic pills and dates blocked off
to see your therapist. but instead, it is me,
i have accepted that it is me.
i have stopped trying to cut it away from me
like one trims split ends, or plucks a single strand
of grey hair. I have come to smile at me wearing it
like a lock of hair behind my left ear.
i am better than you– even with my clinical label –
i am better than you. i am nicer, kinder, stronger,
more rational, more generous.
so, i do not mind living in-sane.
it is better than living in-turmoil,
in-regret, in-tears. my (in)sanity is better than
your sanity and everyone sees it, but you.

Sequence

Summer supple leaves
slowly desiccate.
Edges curl inward
as elderly fingers
furling into palms.

Autumn kisses
Mortality's cheek
and whispers to her
that her time has come.

He recalls each button
through the eyelets
of her blouse, and deflowers
the ribbon of her corset.

Pardoning her ashen
breast, he pauses to take
in the trace of their roundness
and recalls the pleasure
gained during the fastening.

He can't contain his gratification
at the knowledge that nothing is ever lost –
only undone and redone.

Adorned in her lace chemise,
the intricate crisscross
of branches desuetude
of their lively functions,

she is aglow with the embers
of the moment adjacent to a climax,
and she smiles
as she embraces her
deliquescence into Spring.

don't stay dead for too long

…and my blindness
momma always said
*"don't read in the dark,
you'll mess up your eyesight."*
dad, grandpa, someone
– maybe Hindsight,
should have said
*"don't live in the dark shadows
of other people's lives,
you'll distort your view
of them
and of you."*
yeah, maybe that Hindsight
bitch should have told me.

maybe that bitch shoulda
said *"don't get lost
in your lost focus."*
cause i didn't even notice
the wars, the raping,
the world turned upside down.
i didn't stop to console the dying
souls. didn't hear the siren's
sound. i didn't hear my own
deafness. *¿how can you heed
what you can't hear?*
the stiff cold blue bodies – the still,
nearly dead ones too, i looked
past them all. 'twas
sheer, blinding
insanity.

i was staring so intently,
with such intense selectivity
counting the white-shirted
basketball players, that i missed

the witches, the gorillas, the moonwalking
bears; are you sure that they were there
the whole time? was that white horse
galloping behind that dope-ass dancing
there the first time too? rewind.
damn, they all were. right
there, hidden in plain sight.
Hindsight,
time's whore, that filthy
ass whore, has yet again
made a fool of me.

…and my deafness
how can you hear anything
that quiet
with everyone
and everything
screeching at such a deafening
pitch? how is it that the frivolous
spermatozoa, those frivolous
bastards, swim the furthest
the fastest, and are always first
to reach, pierce, and monopolize
the ear?
i bet Hindsight,
time's whore, that filthy
whore bitch
knows the secret
of their slither
oh-so-very-intimately
well.

damn.
i bet she does. bet
she can recite every
perversion,
every single solitary one
that they

lark happily
whispered into her
young, impressionable,
confused and betrayed,
innocent, little ear.

i wonder
who filthed her
skin. who, or what,
turned her inside out,
who taught her
the tricks
that she so expertly
turns, the number of times
it took to get them right,
the pain
of the practice.

hindsight, you bitch
you poor, sad, pitiful
life-sucking bitch, I
cannot believe
that you, so soiled in sin,
have turned me within
and once again have made
a fool, a friend
of me. this must be
(in)sanity.

Part III: Spring

Therapy Work – Appointment #1

January 2nd

Topic: Parental Relationships

1) Do you relate more to your Mother or Father?

I guess, I relate more to my mom than to my dads…

> *¿I wonder if that dominance*
> *and recessiveness is a duality*
> *mostly of nature or nurture,*
> *chance or circumstance,*
> *DNA or day-to-day?*
>
> *I wonder if it is because I'm female*
> *or because all the messed-up shit*
> *with my father figures? I mean,*
> *that shit was complicated.*

I guess, I relate more to my mom than to my dads…
…but I relate to them in ways that stick,
never to be undone. Stick the way movie lines do
because you replay them all the time.

You know, the ones you revisit over
and over and recite with your friends;
the ones that ascend past fame to become immortal
lines in trivia games. The ones that stain you.

The ones that echo the urgent and casual classics –
"Get out of the street!"
"Don't touch the stove!"
"Sure, go ahead, do what you want."
– and by that mere association, you knew
they were something to hold on to.

Knew to uproot the reaction from the current situation,
hold it, and place it into that of another,
study it for contextualization. Infer
that if it riled him up that much, one day
a lesson would be trailing near or far behind.

It's Complicated^1

My birth father ~~was~~, is a rapist.
Since I disowned him,
I don't know which tense applies,
don't know if he's still raping.
don't know if he's still even alive.

The tension of processing
any of this, is so fucking infuriating.
Its pushes and pulls exercise no restraint,
its drips of sweat impose on everything,
even things that should take no hesitation,
like taking headcount for graduation
and longing to hold him a seat…

It's Complicated^2

I've had other dads. Dad_2 tried to fix his
stutter and stammer by frenching dope
in glass crack pipes.

He'd smoke the bill money. Until
Mom started to use what she loved
to protect what she must. To stash that cash,
she hemmed and unhemmed them curtain hems.
I swear, that was the dopest thing I've ever seen.

The shit ended badly. His dope-fiend body
outstretched dead
at the kitchen door.
Scratches on his back, damn –
if only paws could perform CPR.

It's Complicated^3

My final dad is far from perfect, but he moved us
to something resembling normal,
a lesser degree of dysfunction, if nothing else.
Even still, the shit is complicated.

…Complicated like him melting my heart
and me not knowing what to do
with the excess. Then by his example,
learning to keep it.

…Complicated like compound interest, like
saving excess for myself + tending to my best
interest * stacking lessons on top of lessons.

…Complicated like the multiplication and exponentiation
of investment, compassion, and charitable contribution;
learning that when you can't count the number
of times you go to bed hungry, putting all your power
into helping others through a food ministry
leads to never having a pain of hunger again.
(I'm hungry*I'm hungry*I'm
hungry^ the feed the hungry = never hunger again).

…Complicated like simultaneously restoring my faith
in men and strengthening my resolve,
to know that if after we all trudge through
the bowels of hell, only to all wake up there,
I could chisel the ice from my frozen heart,
slip cubes down my throat, and extend the rest
to whomever I choose.

Rooted in Dysfunction

I heard that kid doctors let kids draw pictures
to help process the trauma they can't articulate.
Me, being the cynical deep thinker that I am,
started to imagine my family tree.
It would probably skew and lean heavy to one side
like plant limbs that surpass the others obstructing
their reach towards the pulse of light.

All the crisscrossing, knotting, and tying,
of soul-ties and bloodlines
in the weave of that muthasucka's roots,
is why God hates divorce –
Although, that tree would be quite the sight,
branch ugly, root strong, and…
whatever it wanted to be.

The Body Will Follow the Mind

My dad taught me how to drive.
I don't remember any of our sessions
except that day he yelled
"You ain't got no depth perception!"

Have you ever seen an old-ass, big-ass
four-door, 1980 Lincoln Continental
Mark VI? That car was two sizes too big.
Squarely, it wasn't even a car, it was a blue
boat floating on wheels. It had a long,
long-ass square hood and a long square ass.

It was the length of men in their sixties
reminiscing 'bout their heydays,
winking and waving at a young girl,
eighteen-years of age.

Plus, I was just learning
to handle the wheel.
The math added up –
I was going to hit some shit.
There was no way to avoid it.

It was only a parking lot,
it was only orange cones bending from the wind
squeezed from them. For him,
those cones must have been
curbs, hydrants, or big Mack trucks,
and it was on him to make me skillful,
enough to handle the body
led by any wheel.

Bending the Body

Directly after your reflex and shock,
you may have to bend to collect yourself.
To calm your gasping and panting for breath

...adjacent to your boiling and seething
about the drunken operator of the big Mack truck.
For he and Mack were weaving and weaving
left, right, and center, all about the road,
like he sicced Mack to storm your lane,
to barrel head-on towards you.

...adjacent to your seething and resenting
about how he forced the bending
of your car. Put you in the position
that forced you to swerve,
that forced you to handle the wheel.

...adjacent to your resenting, and unresolve
about how you drove yourself down that road
to go see that boy, to go do that thing
that you weren't supposed to be doing.

That you were where you weren't supposed to be.
That you put yourself in that place –
where you weren't supposed to be.

That there you are, wrecked, but alive
on the cusp of adjacency.

You may have to bend to avoid
hitting your head when maneuvering
through old, antiquated, cellared spaces.
Just remember to undo your bend,
rise, and straighten again
once you have made it through
the clearing.

You may have to bend, stretch your arms like wings,
gather the things that you hold closest to your heart –
that you'd release rather than sword splice apart.
Incubate with as much force as you can,
propel yourself upright like a mighty pillar of light
with five generations beaming right through you.
A shattered ceiling all around you.

Yet again, you may have to bend to entertain
a small child gleefully flashing
the coins of her own earning
from the sale of her lemonade.

My dad said, *"always remember –
trees that bend withstand the wind."*

You
    may
     have
    to
bend.

Not Left Unburied

November 11th

We used to watch guerrilla warfare movies.
Saw soldiers draw straws to win or lose unwanted duties.
Saw their boots transverse the bowels of hell
and their bodies get blown apart.
Saw ones that survived, by fate or luck of the draw,
bellow the deepest, most noiseless, guttural sounds
that can fit into the space of
  "three seconds, MOVE NOW!"
…to summons strength for exertion,
give it time to parallel fortitude.
…to gather brothers over shoulders –
first slinging the arms that are still attached,
then wrapping around hips to heave torsos over.
…to carry their wounded.
The heaviness of each soldier's weight
worthy of getting him to a place,
that would permit him the space
for all to breathe
the thin, pregnant, laborious air of awaiting
prospective surviving or dying a death
punctuated by decency of burial. To inter him,
mark his entrance to eternity
with simple formality
of decent introduction.

No matter what, *"Thank you for your service, Dad."*

Therapy Work – Appointment #2

January 9th

Topic: Depth Perception

1) You mentioned a memory that stuck with you. Read the following passage. What thoughts does it prompt?

> Each eye reports the depiction that it gathers. The brain melds both reports together into one full picture. For most people this happens so seamlessly, and with such ease, that they are unaware that it happens.
>
> Somethings are best unfolded through phrases and stories. Like the saying about there being three sides to every story – yours, mine, and the truth – no one is lying, the truth has elements of both. *¡Facts, unless one of us is a habitual liar or sociopath!*
>
> Or that fable about the father who sent each of his four children to view a tree, each sent in a different season, each coming back with their own account that they stick by because they saw it with their own eyes. Each separate account, only a partial view of the full picture.

I see a lot here. One thing that speaks are the lessons
that I learned from both of my parents. Their combined wisdom
allowed me to reach deep perception.
Usually, stories are deeper than what you first see.

Therapy Work – Appointment #3

January 16th

Topic: Spatial Awareness

1) Read the following passage. What does it say to you? Think about how you see yourself.

> Have you ever sized-up other people and their accomplishments and then compared yourself to them? Sure, most of us do this all the time. Have you ever been walking in a crowded space and turned sideways to pass someone to avoid running into them? Sure, most of us do this all the time too. Does it surprise you that these two processes are connected? *¡Raises hand!*

> Our minds collect and analyze information about ourselves and about objects in our environment to gauge our physical, emotional, and spiritual proximity to those objects…for our protection and survival. We are subconsciously aware of how much space we occupy for the purpose of safely navigating around other people and things to avoid hitting them and causing harm or damage.

> Benchmarking serves the purpose of assessing the relation between you and other people or things to determine if you are in danger and to avoid collisions, that is it. Do not take this natural mental process beyond this purpose.

> Do not internalize any negative feelings of inferiority, self-doubt, or envy. Keep this natural mental process in check, limited to its intended purpose, and you will preserve your energy. You will feed and sustain your positive energy; you will maintain your focus and feel motivated. You

will eliminate spending time feeling bad about yourself; you will starve negative energy that would only drain you and leave you unmotivated.
¡Yeah, starve that love-starved shit!

The secret: Do not beat yourself up past the point of assessing danger, if you can clear the object, it is all good, keep moving forward.

*So, my awareness of my body is natural. I see myself.
I am supposed to see myself. I judge myself. I am supposed to judge myself. But not in the way that I've been force-fed on social media and TV.*

It's not about being too big or too small, too fat or too skinny, light- or dark-skinned. I should mind my body only enough to not crash into someone or something else.

Double Dutch

I'm talking that cable rope Double Dutch,
the kind that I grew up watching in the seventies and eighties.
The whole experience a concerted event,
a mystical swirl of air stirring music and cathartic release.

It is amazing to see what these turners and jumpers
can do with their bodies, it is a sight to behold,
supernatural. These girls whip ropes so fast, they warp time.
Revolutions spin the Earth in seconds not days,
and minutes instead of years.

Two turners keep the tempo,
turning ropes with every joint of their arms
– wrists, elbows, shoulders –
and each bone and muscle in between,
giving a good whipping in reverse. These girls
work hard as hell, as hard as the jumpers.

One, or as many that can get in, jump, pound, stomp
inside the turn of the rope, jackhammering
the pavement of their concrete jungles.
They transverse through the rope's orbit
with ease, and if they must wait to catch the break
of the whips, they rock back and forth shifting
their weight from one leg to the other.

Always aware – of the timing of the ropes,
of the other girls, of the stopwatch
to break records for speed,
of the practiced routine,
because there are marks that need to be hit.

Double Dutching is a great way to pass time
when there ain't nothing else to do,
cause momma ain't got no money,
and the world ain't got no patience for people
that look like you.

Funny that it's called Double Dutch, cause like
double Dutch, it is an unintelligible
language to some. To us, it is ingenious
and familiar like indigenous. At times,
it is the most articulate option we have.

Trying Out Black Girl Magic

The ropes sting if they catch you.
The sting of cable on shins
feels like switches of punishment,
reminding us to keep our grades up,
so we don't get cut from the team.

Coach talks a lot about honing
spatial awareness, how to perceive
our bodies in relation to the ropes, judge
their speed, watch intently for windows
to jump in, on faith at first,
but eventually on skill.

We must make split-second
decisions to wait or rush in,
so we become disciples of focus
and discipline. The body follows
the mind through the eyes, so
taking your eyes off the prize
will set you adrift. Losing focus
at high speed, high stake games,
is detrimental given shortened
recovery windows.

For us, this is more than a game,
this is our ticket to thrive.
So, on the day we face dream-dashing
cuts, we bow to our knees
and sing songs for who those
who will not make the cut.

Egyptian Vine

Our people have always been ingenious.
Our people have always been a collective.
It shows in our recreational pastimes,
like the swinging of Egyptian vine.

When there is one vine and two girls, one
does not have to sit out —— simply,
each hold one end and begin
to swing in tandem, jump together,
land together, laugh and have fun together.

When there are three or more girls, still
no one is left out, nobody is left to sit alone
by themselves and pout —— simply,
let one girl hold the pair of ends,
loop the middle of the vine around the waist
of another, and begin to swing in sync. Swing
both sides of the vine toward or away
from the other, and let the other girls jump in.

When there is one girl by herself, just her
and that one long vine – she will
simply double it and begin to jump, land, laugh,
and have fun on her own.

Polyglot

Spirit speaks in any language Spirit wants.
Spirit resonates quick within,
like the quickening of ancestral
lines, and the intervening spaces
between. Bearing witness to Egyptian vine
swinging is to witness witnesses witnessing.

These witnesses transfer all forms of matter
through spry springing of shoe tongues.

These witnesses transcribe, through
the churning axels of their wrists,
the goings-on … a'going-on.

The bodies of these witnesses rock-sway
back and forth in queue to enter in;
pressing the Earth to bind and loose
while they wait for signal of return.

These witnesses decipher the transmission
of ethereal code through depth-perceiving eyes.

These witnesses circuit circadian days
in seconds. For not all time is the same.
One day of Spirit is as one thousand days for man.

These witnesses –
the vines, and the interstices between,
the stirring air, the prophets, the scribes, the interceders,
the seers, the musicians, the timekeepers –
all alternate in rhythmic intervals.
Role by role, converse in synchronous
dialogue, gloriously ushering Spirit.

Spirit understands any language Spirit wants.
Yet, spirit's pass is limited; for not all spirit is the same.
There is but one language foreign to the ear of God,
the one of the people that She will no longer hear
when She says … *"Depart from Me."*

The braiding of coiled hair,
is yet another language. It is exquisite
conversations between deities
in the openness of ether. Have you
ever seen the moves of their fingers? I perceive,
they are sign language telegraphing Spirit.

Double Entendre

I am a polyglot.
Fluent in many languages,
such as double Dutch.
That must be the root cause
of them deeming me unintelligible,
and becoming so off-put by my babble
that they refuse to invite me to the room,
let alone offer me a seat at the table.
My words are just gibberish to their ears.

I must speak too much, doublespeak,
too much. Must have publically reveled
in the revelation of one too many mysteries,
one too many times, and got myself
and my mysterious words rebuffed
like private things with no business
in public places.

Banished ingeniousness,
dwelling in the isolation of genius,
stumbles to the hum of its seclusion,
never ceasing to form hypotheses
that over time prove to be theorems.

Part IV: Summer

Interlude

We be groovin' on a vibe
so right, so in line
The mind alone cannot master
the feelings,
the way I be feeling you
it is something brand new

It is the difference between
a recipe
and smelling the flavor,
tasting the succulent meat
so juicy that you have to wipe
the sides of your mouth

You've got it Baby
Whatever it is
you've got it
Oh Baby, Baby,
Yes, you do

Juke Joint Gospel

Just like an 11x13 print –
blues, reds, yellows, and greens
vibrant and alive –
hug ladies' rear ends,
rotund and shapely like trunks of old cars.

Coordinating hats –
large and flamboyant –
shade three quarters of their faces,
like windshield sun visors pulled down.

Fans in hand –
waving wildly –
in sync with the rhythm,
but do nothing to cool the steamy air down.

The energy is high,
everyone is having a good time,
the shack/sanctuary is full of life and vigor.

The slurring of speech, the speaking in tongues,
swaying, clapping, slapping thighs,
loud shouts, grunts, and fits of possession.

Tap your foot,
wave your hand,
groove freely to the sultry notes
of the live band.

The choir, the organist, the jukebox record.
Vinyl, live, it is all the same.
The juke joint, the morning service.

Dispense

I'm his pharmacist.
Whenever he needs
to relax,
to relate,
to release,
he comes a' looking
for me.
When he tired
he comes for me.
When he stressed
he comes for me.
When he longs, he comes
only for me.

I deal
dopamine, oxytocin,
serotonin. melatonin,
melanin, motivation,
scolding admonishment,
and loving adoration. I deal
him whatever he needs.

I fix
him. I fix
his neurons, I fix
his synapses. I
fix his broken,
too washed out,
too stressed out to fire
emasculated
impotence.
I ignite
his fire.

I am his pharmacist
and I dispense to him
only, only whatever
we need.

Junkie

I know a poet who is on that stuff,
always rummaging around
for her next hit.
She tramps into shadowy corners
scooping-up handfuls
of blackness; slighting her wrists up
studying all its shades of opaqueness; closing
her eyes, undivided attention to
the
  feeling
    of
    it
      falling
        through
         the
          breaks
           of her fingers.

I know a poet who is on that stuff.
She slips on the silk gown of nightfall, shakes stars
in her hands like dice, and tosses them
        air.
     the
   in
up

Then closes one eye, narrows
the other, and plucks
them
one
by
one
with jeweler's tweezers.

Sorting them by color and clarity,
she places them
in small black velvet
bags with drawstrings until

they are all tucked away,
and the sky is clear, and black
velvety with drawstring streaks
along the horizon.

Yeah, I know a poet who is on that stuff
and she sho nuff has it bad.

Old English

I thought…
"They just don't make them like they used to…"
Then I found you…
Eyes open wide, feeling good inside…
Lying in the bed, drunk sober…
40 ounces to the head, Old English…
3 pounds in me now, I need this!!!

Dipsomaniac now, no temperance…
I'm dranking your sober…
My eyes dranking, ears dranking…
lips dranking, my body dranking…
Flooding my mind with inebriations…
so, soooo intoxicated!!!

It's real…
You so real, so sober…
This drunken sobriety is the shit!!!
And you let me hit,
over and over…

It is that Old-time English, way back
old school…
Crown me royal, Steven me…
I crown you king, reciprocity…
I'm made for you, be with me…
Only for you, believe in me…
We triumphant, victory…
I'm your Seven, you're my Three.

Cannabis Brown

He sat in the back of class,
quiet, never really contributing much.

Until one day when Mrs. Jackson
had our class break into small groups
and each share a poem that we had written.

Kelly Hobson droned on about shopping sprees
on her father's credit card, and Luke Green
went all Sci-Fi about drones.

Mitchell Blake had a poem full of clichés
that he swore was the pinnacle of original,
while mine was just okay.

But Cannabis Brown's was so deft that today
his poem I can still remember:

At each day's end
I tether daylight
until it is typewriter threaded
between both thumbs and index fingers.

I fold the horizon over itself,
over itself, over itself,
furling it into a perfect joint.

I press one end into the sun.
With each drag, the firmament crackles
shades of red and orange.

Persimmon, sangria, amber,
and terra cotta consensually
mate their edges like copulating
earthworms until ash grey climax
canopies the sky.

And the people high by contact
devour dinner to curb their munchies,
slouch on couches reefer lazy,
and draw their drapes for the evening
on the roach black night.

Momma's Gifts

My mother told me that she saw
a pair of praying hands in the sky at the time of my birth.
Momma is like that, predisposed to visions…
able to decipher dreams… inclined to interpret tongues.

Growing up in the presence of such gifts
was like having fruit-yielding trees planted
in our backyard.

Momma's mom's mom had sown trees of wisdom and faith.
These trees were passed down to Momma for safekeeping.

My baby sister and I watched Momma
water those trees with her tears; speak to them
with prayer, praise, and worship; prune them
with rebukes of the enemy; and salve them with anointing oil.

She taught us how to pick fruit from the trees.
How to always wash the fruit
with the cleansing water of understanding
before putting it to mouth.

It seemed like Momma had an affinity
for the fruit of the faith tree.
My baby sister and I, following in her footsteps
raided that tree more often than the other.

We would zealously pick the peach-like fruit
at the height of its ripeness, place it under
the backyard spigot, and rinse-off the itchiness of its down.

Biting cheek-deep, the nectar would slip down our necks
and between our fingers. And we would be ready
for another before our last bites.

One day, though not abandoning our faithful peaches,
my baby sister and I, also having an acquired taste for wisdom,
each picked a crisp, crunchy apple-like fruit. **99**

We washed it with understanding,
and took a seat under that tree's protectiveness,
our backs up against its sturdiness.

We labored to chew each bite to completion.
Grinding the fruit until its texture became simple
enough to swallow, to digest.

Having the time to think, we received the revelation
of Momma's "affinity" for faith. It wasn't that she was all
faith and little wisdom, but rather the contrary.

Wisdom, requiring much work to obtain, provides great satiety.
The mind locks in the taste of its bittersweetness,
never letting go of its lessons.

Whereas faith, easily bruised by disappointments and setbacks
fades faster and needs building-up more often.

And we thank Momma for the gifts that she gave us,
the trees rooted in our own backyards.
The ones from which our children now apple and peach pick.

Rituals

If you would have been born in Egypt,
relatives and friends would have come to see you
at seven days of age. Your mother and I would have decorated
the house with lit candles, flowers, and fruits.

Had you have been born in Kenya,
your mother would have strapped you to her back
and brought you to the thorn enclosure where the
cattle live. There I would have given you your name.

Finding My Name

Since I was five, I have been searching
for my name. Momma told me
that I had one that was solely mine,
a gift from some man upstairs.

She said that things that do not speak
with mouths already know it.
The water that babbles and spits over
smooth rocks knows my name.

The underfoot crush of grass,
of snow, knows my name. The long
quiet of leaves redressing from green
to plum and brown knows my name.

And they speak it aloud all the time.
She said that I'd have to train my ear
to hear it because they proclaim many
names in harmony.

She said that while my fists were small,
my name would be hidden in the smiles
of rainbows in oil slicks, and in the breath
between butterflies' wings.

She said that when my fists were skilled
enough to hold water
without losing it,
I'd find my name.

I think I have found my name.
I have finally opened my fists,
holding water with two cupped palms.
For everything I use both my head
and my heart, and they are open
enough, and closed enough to hold
substance. I think I have found my name.

Someone to Lead Us

You have truly found your place
in this swirl of laughter and tears.
You know who you are.
You walk with a stride that shows
that you know your purpose,
that you know where to be
and what to be doing at every moment.
Your laugh is as free as ripples and eagles.
Your smile is as brilliant as shining gems.

Quintessence[0]

When I pass by
I flutter like a butterfly flying
in the Shanghai blue sky.

When I pass by
people stop and take a glance.
When I pass by
people are entranced by my butterfly dance.

When I pass by
boys become liquefied.
When I pass by
sinners repent and cry.

When I pass by
people are awe-struck at my femininity.
When I pass by
people believe they behold in their eyes
a glance of divinity.

When I pass by
people see a rose in full bloom.
When I pass by
people move and make room.

When I pass by
these are the things about me
that people automatically know:

I am fantasy and reality meeting,
where the latter is superseding.

I am the current event that remains
front page news.

I am the one in purple while the rest
are dressed in their blues.

I am mind, body, and soul.
I am diamond birthed from coal.

When I pass by
I think of harmony among all the races.
When I pass by
I smile back at all the smiling faces.

Quintessence[1]

My essence is pleasant.
In my presence you stand immovable,
entranced by my stance,
by my dance. With one glance
you become high, become liquefied.
I have the golden eye that will make you cry.
Make you say damn if I die, myself I crucify,
before I look dead eye at the bullseye
and still let you sweet butterfly
blow by in the Shanghai blue sky.

I have a sapphire empire that burns
desire like wildfire. Sitting
by a campfire taking long, cool
champagne sips…
making your hotwire trip…

I gently caress you,
and you fondle my hair, lips, and face.
You touch my soft skin, and you want
to plunge in, but you wait…
and once again rearrange
my silk, satin, and lace.

You stand awe-struck at my femininity.
Your eyes behold a brief glance of divinity,
so close in the vicinity, that you forget
my virginity and crave infinite masculinity.

You commence to meditate on your offense
to lubricate my mind, medicate my
well-defined behind, and penetrate I,
the epitome of womankind. The genuine artifact,
an ancient relic preserved.

You say you have sought
and not found…until now…
Here I stand in full bloom.

I am your fantasy and reality meeting,
where the latter is superseding.
I am the current event that remains
front page news.
I am the one in purple when the rest
are dressed in their blues.
I am mind, body, and soul,
crystalline carbon birthed from pressured coal,
I am His embodiment personified,
I am *Quintessential.*

This Is a Love Poem – Sort of

I have been struggling to write a love poem.
It has just occurred to me that maybe
the reason this is so hard for me to do is –
I have never been in love.

I have lost love, had painful love, failed love,
but never simply, lasting love.

I just want to be able to tell someone that
"Our love is as full as the ocean touching
the seams of the horizon afar."
But I fall short each time.

Instead, I am rutted in the lines of:
"You'll do for now"
"We're ... adventurous"
"You're my experiment in charity"
"Don't get comfortable"
"Were as passionate as an exhibit
that rolled into town, exciting, but ending soon"
"I have on my short-range glasses with you –
I don't see a future"

No matter how hard I try, I just can't pretty up those phrases.
They just don't sound as poetic as,
"Our love is as full as the ocean touching
the seams of the horizon afar."

Sweet Nothings

His whispered sweet nothings
were bitter every-things.
Go to hell. You
and your twisted tongue.
This space is reserved
for the one who's
sweet every-things
leave me
tongue-tied.

Journey's Rain

Our journey is like the diary of rain.

Our love is from the stratosphere
high above the Earth,
like the nimbostratus
which unashamedly
gives birth.

Each bead is a hope
of possibility, reciting
our exploration of love.

We are brand new
You to I, and I to you.
We are fresh, green,
unpolluted brand new.

Each drop of rain wishes
to hopefully reunite
with some aspect of Mother Earth.
Just as we desire
to return to the womb
of our birth.

Is my womb your garden
for you to continue
to grow? In you
will I be returning home?

What experiences
and feelings will we have
along the way? What
is in store for us
at the end of the day?

Like the rain wonders
to what surface will it inescapably
plummet, we wonder
how our journey will end.

A raindrop can land
on the slick, smooth back
of a seal, or on the brash mossy
bark of a maple tree. It could
whimsically join the race
among its own kind
down the windshield
of a silver Infiniti.
It could excitedly enter
the enthralling escapade
of a clear puddle awaiting
a child's rainy-day play.

Will we continue
to fellowship as smoothly
as that seal's back?
Will we agree
to disagree
peacefully?
Will we share
whimsically innocent
moments like those
of a child at play?

Rain comes to life
when I think of you.

I think of you
and I think of rain.
Falling, frolicking, trembling,
tumbling, thundering, drenching
consuming me.

Two Step (Pas de Deux II)

Polite_bones @Bone_deep
#Mood #IsSmiling
WhenYouFeelAwfulLike–
PuttingOnPerfumeWhenYouAreFunky?

Bone_deep @Polite_bones LOL!!!
Hey Babe. I don't think so.
You feeling okay?

Yeah, I'm fine, just thinking.
The thing about me is I never think
the worst – the worst never enters
my mind – until it happens,
and then I wearily realize
that I must keep my eyes open.

Sometimes you know
even when you don't
know that you know.

That part!

You need a hug?

You are so sweet.

I try.

You know what seems odd to me?
Fear of clowns. I'm wondering if
I should fear rainbows. They are
supposed to be a reassurance that
God will never flood
the Earth new again.
#FeelingLikeDoOversAreTheRightIdea

Damn.

****

Bone_deep @Polite_bones
How was your day?

Polite_bones @Bone_deep
Productive.

That's dope! What did you do?

Ran, cleaned my kitchen, wrote,
went to the protest.

Shit! I saw that on TV.
I'm glad your safe.
Riot gear? I mean, is
that shit really necessary?
We just want to be heard.

Flat out. I mean the shit has gotta
stop for it to be the past, right?
If the shit is still being done,
and if we are still looking at the shit
right now, then WTF can anyone
expect?

That part! Say that shit again
louder for the people in the back!

LOL!!! Exactly!!! How was
your day?

#Mood
#DesiringToMake
GreatDecisionsForTheFuture–
NotJustOkayOnesForToday

113

That's dope!

You coming over tonight?

Not sure. I gotta study for this final exam. Plus, I'm in a zone. Thinking I might get some sleep, then get up early tomorrow and tend to my garden. It's supposed to be nice.

#Respect.
You'll still be with me tonight though, cause I'mma think about you all night long.

😊 *Good night.*

Good night. Love you.

I love you too.

****

Bone_deep: @Polite_bones
Good Morning My Love!

Polite_bones: @Bone_deep
Good Morning My Love.
Just think, in the future, there will be new colors; ones that exist but were previously undetected.

Wow, like beyond ultraviolet? What sparked that thought?

Not sure, just morning inspiration,
I guess. Yes, colors that are beyond
the spectrum of what the naked
human eye can detect. And
pigments in nature
that have yet to be cultivated.

So, I can give you that rainbow?

LMFAO!!!! I'm laughing so hard!
I almost spit out my tea!

The Difference is You

For my now Husband

If I offered you a bare book,
and invited you to join me in filling its pages
with memories
to reminisce on thirty years from now.
What would you do?

I have a feeling that you would pause,
thinking through every potential pleasure,
pitfall, joy, and ramification.

I think that ultimately, you would accept,
knowing that we are more often happier
than not. At least that is what I think
that you would do, but I am still getting
to know you.

Although I am getting to know you more,
this one thing I know for sure…

My life is different now, and that difference
is you. I had a suitor in my life before, but
that plaintiff brought nothing in my life but war.
He brought pain, abuse, grief, distress, and unrest.

God saw fit to heal my pain through someone
who answers to the same name.
There is one huge difference, and that difference is you.

You are so special to me
and I love you dearly. Clearly
with you, there is understanding,
communication, truth, trust
unity, success, and hugs,
between us.

So after one week
turns into one month,
turns into one year,
turns into thirty,
we'll be rocking in chairs
holding hands, viewing the book
that we've shared a lifetime
filling with love.

You will call me
your wife.
You will still be the love
of my life.
You will be my best friend.
You will still hold my hand.
You will know me
as well as I know myself.
Together we will have amassed
great wealth.

So from now, to then, and beyond…
Hold me when I need
a friend. Kiss me when
you do not want the night
to end. Love me, even when
I am wrong.
Listen to me and hear
my unique song.

Place your heart into my care,
knowing that I will certainly
be there. I will do the same
for you. I will be
your difference too.

Marriage

Our tongue-kissing
leaves us tongue-tied
like souls tied
to promises that are virtuous and good.

The Pretty You Make

There she is. Lovely,
like porcelain.
Glazed, polished, translucently opaque.
With a golden clasp
pursing two fire-baked lips
sealed
airtight.

She is regal, poised, ornate.
Seemingly solely ceremonial.
What purpose does a box like this really serve?
To look pretty whilst encasing things that look pretty?

Secrets uneasy inside her belly.
Gone down bitter
acquainted the elixir
deep, deep, down inside her.
Elixir, confusion, joy
confusion, elixir, pain
elixir, confusion, anger
mixed-up.
She so mixed-up,
she so shook,
that she just shook, and shook, and shook.
She turned to book.
She turned to pen.
She turned to taste
her own elixir within.
She turned
mixologist,
she found some grit,
and she shook, shook, shook, shook that shit.

Secrets rest easy inside her belly.
Gone down bitter,
rise up tender, and
only, only rise to
center

between her
painted lips
when she beckons
them.
She parts her golden mouth
when she chooses.
She unlatches her lips,
and relieves them of their guard.

Secrets rise
pretty
and pull
pull
pour
from inside
her
like the
pretty
pretty
pearled
choker
that
wraps
the neck
of her
pretty,
seemingly
solely
ceremonial,
vessel
of
clay.

Things That Fit into a Small Child's Palm

My pride.
The number of fucks given for anything that no longer serves me.
My own laughter singing in my ears.
A shiny new coin.

I finally woke up
like girl, you still *wishing*
for days
when *your* contentment can fit
into a small palm
like a shiny new coin?

Girl, you are doing it wrong.
Everything in life is a choice. Drive the damn car.
Live life like Monday is more
than just a stitch of time between Sunday and Tuesday.
Own your autonomy, rent everything else.
Own your autonomy, be tethered to nothing else.

I finally woke up

I finally woke up
like girl,

I finally woke up
like girl, you still *wishing*

I finally woke up
like girl, you still *wishing*
for days

I finally woke up
like girl, you still *wishing*
for days
when *your* contentment can fit

I finally woke up
like girl, you still *wishing*
for days
when *your* contentment can fit
into a small palm
like a shiny new coin?

Girl, you are doing it wrong.
Everything in life is a choice. Drive the damn car.
Live life like Monday is more
than just a stitch of time between Sunday and Tuesday.
Own your autonomy, rent everything else.
Own your autonomy, be tethered to nothing else.

I finally woke up
like girl,
Yes or No
Stay or Go
Do or Don't
Heads or Tails
The shit is simple.

You know what fits into a tiny palm?
Two words.
A shiny, two-sided coin.
Choice.
Choice always fits into a tiny palm.

Choose
Choose *your* autonomy, rent everything else.
Choose *your* autonomy, be tethered to nothing
be
    tethered
        to
            nothing
                else.

Who Is Henna Quill?

Henna Quill is a poet and inspired being. She is a mixture of mind, body, and spirit – and she pours each part of her into her poetry. Henna's work is about her readers, it is purposed to plant seeds of awakening, choice, and autonomy, which in turn stir drafts of liberation. None of us get everything right every time, and we are not supposed to. We are supposed to live, learn, and hold both our wins and our losses. Living life in a way that arcs towards balance is healthy and obtainable. This is Henna's truth, and she shares this truth with her audiences in untainted, raw, and refined poetry that provokes thought and action. Choose, Live, Be.

Henna Quill is also a product of exposure to poverty, mental illness, domestic violence, and abuse. She is a product of lovingly and frustratingly parenting brilliant children with unique considerations, singly for twenty-five years. She is a product of a deeply prayerful and faithful family. She is the product of rising above trauma and despair, to shape her life into what she deems it to be. She chooses to be internally driven, educated, kind, and optimistic.

Henna Quill pinpoints that her longing for a relationship came from society – it was external pressure from an external construct that she internalized. Henna eventually understood the need to, and liberation in, de-subscribing from the linear corridors that many societies shove us into; and how this linear thinking extends beyond relationships into most aspects of life including beauty, motherhood, fatherhood, work life imbalance, career options, education, race, religion, gender, health, lifestyle, politics, disability, personality, etc. To all this Henna says – Choose your autonomy, be tethered to nothing, be tethered to nothing else.

CPSIA information can be obtained
at www.ICGtesting.com
Printed in the USA
LVHW010405140321
681277LV00001B/1